THE REPUBLICAN PART`

CHAPTER ONE

The Republican Party was formed in 1854 with the intention of abolishing slavery permanently in the United States and to help the black men, women and children in this country.

Although it would be several months until it was official, with its first political candidate, the unofficial birth of the Republican Party is widely considered to have been on March 20, 1854. It was on that day that a group of brave Americans gathered together at Ripon, Wisconsin.

That is when the first time that the name, "Republican" was uttered.

These men had enough of the atrocities that were going on against black people in this country, and knew that it was time to make a stand.

The final straws were the Democrats strict

enforcement of the 1950 Fugitive Slave Act and the imminent passage of the Kansas-Nebraska Act.

A bill for the latter was introduced in January 1854 by Democratic Senator Stephen Douglas and was fiercely supported by President Franklin Pierce (also a Democrat).

The writing was on the wall that the Kansas-Nebraska Act would make it through Congress and soon become a law.

Prior to the formation of the Republican Party, tensions were brewing to a boiling point thanks to the Southern Democrats and one of the most divisive Presidents ever, the aforementioned, President Franklin Pierce.

Despite being a New England Democrat, he possessed many of the ideals of Southern Democrats, including being pro-slavery.

At the time of his election in 1852 many in the country were becoming anti-slavery, but this wasn't the case in the Democratic Party.

While some Northerners in the party were becoming more open to abolishing slavery, a few were becoming strongly opposed to it, whereas the majority (especially in the south) were firmly entrenched in the abomination.

Pierce fooled many of the Northern Democrats who wanted to end the practice and unite the country while assuring the Southern Democrats (including the slave owners) that he was on their side.

After winning the election of 1852, everyone saw his true colors, as well as a majority of the Democrats that were around.

His hatred and utter disdain for black people, particularly slaves, would become evident in many ways, but specifically his strict application of the 1850 Fugitive Slave Act and the passing of the Kansas-Nebraska Act.

The results of his decisions would lead the United States on a perilous one-way path to an inevitable Civil War.

At the time Pierce was elected, there was a bit of relative calmness between the North and the South, as recent tensions had eased.

Voters hoped that he could continue this trend, especially at a time when more people were coming around to the idea that the abomination called slavery was barbaric and needed to end.

Pierce, however did not feel this way, and his policies and actions showed the truly racist abhorrent human being that he was.

From his strict enforcement of the 1850 Fugitive Slave Act to the passing of the Kansas–Nebraska Act, and so much more, his despicable self is indefensible.

In 1850, the previous administration, under Millard Fillmore, passed an updated version of the 1793

Fugitive Slave Act. This was passed basically to appease the Southern slave owners as it was very lightly enforced.

On June 29, 2023, the History.com website updated their synopsis of the original 1793 version of the Fugitive Slave Act.

In it they said,

'Despite the inclusion of the Fugitive Slave Clause in the U.S. Constitution, anti-slavery sentiment remained high in the North throughout the late 1780s and early 1790s, and many petitioned Congress to abolish the practice outright.

Bowing to further pressure from Southern lawmakers—who argued the slave debate was driving a wedge between the newly created states—Congress passed the Fugitive Slave Act of 1793.

This edict was similar to the Fugitive Slave Clause in many ways, but included a more detailed description of how the law was to be put into practice. Most importantly, it decreed that owners of enslaved people and their "agents" had the right to search for escapees within the borders of free states.

In the event they captured a suspected runaway, these hunters had to bring them before a judge and provide evidence proving the person was their property. If court officials were satisfied by their proof—which often took the form of a signed affidavit—the owner would be permitted to take custody of the enslaved person and return to their home state. The law also imposed a $500 penalty on any person who helped harbor or conceal escapees.

The Fugitive Slave Act of 1793 was immediately met with a firestorm of criticism. Northerners bristled at the idea of turning their states into a stalking ground for bounty hunters, and many argued the law was tantamount to legalized kidnapping. Some abolitionists organized clandestine resistance groups and built complex networks of safe houses to aid enslaved people in their escape to the North.

Refusing to be complicit in the institution of slavery, most Northern states intentionally neglected to enforce the law. Several even passed so-called "Personal Liberty Laws" that gave accused runaways the right to a jury trial and also protected free blacks, many of whom had been abducted by bounty hunters and sold into slavery.'

History.com also added this very important bit of information that resulted from the original Act, "The passage of the Fugitive Slave Acts resulted in many free blacks being illegally captured and sold into slavery. One famous case concerned Solomon Northup, a freeborn black musician who was kidnapped in Washington, D.C. in 1841. Northup would spend 12 years enslaved in Louisiana before winning back his freedom in 1853."

One would think that with many minds shifting away from the concept of slavery that by 1850, this law would be abolished instead of being enhanced.

But the lawmakers were more interested in not ruffling the feathers of the southern slave owners, so they formed their own, and even worse version of the law.

Although the updated 1850 version, which was part of the "1850 Compromise", was more for appeasing the Southern slave owners, they did like having that piece of paper. Meanwhile, the Northern States didn't like the new law, but put up very little protest at the beginning as there was little enforcement of the law.

Britannica had this to say about the new 1850 version,

"The demand from the South for more effective legislation resulted in enactment of a second Fugitive Slave Act in 1850. Under this law fugitives could not testify on their own behalf, nor were they permitted a trial by jury. Heavy penalties were imposed upon federal marshals who refused to enforce the law or from whom a fugitive escaped; penalties were also imposed on individuals who helped slaves to escape. Finally, under the 1850 act, special commissioners were to have concurrent jurisdiction with the U.S. courts in enforcing the law."

There was a swift response that came from Pierce's strict endorsement of this repulsive law that prior to the Pierce Presidency was enforced about as often as a driver today going 56 in a 55 MPH highway.

His obsessive strictness to carry out every detail of this law was one of the actions from President Pierce that would change this country forever.

His desire to assist the Southern slave owners, while simultaneously taking away the last sliver of hope and dignity from the escaped slaves, led to more dangerous work for the underground railroad as the penalties to assist the escaped slaves dramatically increased.

Pierce didn't care that free backs were often caught without documentation showing that they were in fact free slaves and sold into slavery despite actually being free. He didn't care that many of these included women and children.

Pierce was about as heartless and evil as a man could be.

His actions did come to a boil however, with among other things, such as the case of escaped slaves such as Anthony Burns, and others, as well as riots across the country, and more.

More on those to come, but first another of his disastrous decisions was giving the green light to the Kansas-Nebraska Act.

This new law extended the slavery line in the United States which was like throwing gasoline onto the building fire that was the inflamed emotions of many northerners.

A Britannica article on July 24, 2023, explained it as,

"Kansas-Nebraska Act, officially An Act to Organize the Territories of Nebraska and Kansas, in the antebellum period of U.S. history, critical national policy change concerning the expansion of slavery into the territories, affirming the concept of popular sovereignty over congressional edict. In 1820 the Missouri Compromise had excluded slavery from that part of the Louisiana Purchase (except Missouri) north of the 36°30' parallel. The Kansas-Nebraska Act, sponsored by Democratic Sen. Stephen A. Douglas, provided for the territorial organization of Kansas and Nebraska under the principle of popular sovereignty, which had been applied to New Mexico and Utah in the Compromise of 1850. Pres. Franklin Pierce signed An Act to Organize the Territories of Nebraska and Kansas into law on May 30, 1854.

Written in an effort to arrest the escalating sectional controversy over the extension of slavery, the Kansas-Nebraska Act ironically fanned the flame of national division. It was attacked by free-soil and antislavery factions as a capitulation to the proponents of slavery. Passage of the act was followed by the establishment of the Republican Party as a viable political organization opposed to the expansion of slavery into the territories. In the Kansas Territory a migration of proslavery and antislavery factions, seeking to win control for their respective institutions, resulted in a period of political chaos and bloodshed."

Just days before this law was passed, Pierce's hateful earlier decision of the strict enforcement of the Fugitive Slave Law which had already caused outrage amongst many in the North was greatly exacerbated with the capture of escaped slave, Anthony Burns.

The aftermath of President Pierce's egregious decision to strictly enforce the Fugitive Slave Act should have been predictable, but unfortunately Pierce was blinded by his hatred and contempt for blacks and slaves.

Many times free blacks were caught with the presumption that they were escaped slaves. If they had proper documentation it was just another undignified moment in their lives, however if they had no documentation proving my that they were free blacks then often they were either sent to where these in charge thought they came from or sold into slavery.

This was one of many problems that derived from Pierce's odious decision.

Because of the stiffer penalties for helping escaped slaves many erred on the side of caution, such as those previously mentioned.

In many of their minds they were protecting their families because if those blacks were escaped slaves and they refused to help to turn them in then they would most likely be arrested.

So to many of them, it made no difference if the

blocks were slaves or not, they were turned in with the presumption that they were guilty.

In this case, presumption of innocence went out the window thanks to President Pierce.

The historic underground railroad also had a more difficult time, as less people were willing to help them due to the stiffer penalties if caught.

Fortunately, this didn't stop this brave freedom fighters, as they continued their efforts to help every slave that they could escape to freedom.

THE REPUBLICAN PARTY: FORMED IN 1854 TO END SLAVER...

CHAPTER TWO

There was such tension that had never been seen since the founding of this country.

Things boiled over in May of 1854 with the false arrest of Anthony Burns.

From the website of the "New England Historical Society",

'On the night of May 24, 1854, federal marshals seized 19-year-old Anthony Burns on Court Street and wrestled him into the courthouse on a trumped-up charge of jewelry theft.

Burns was born into slavery in Virginia. When he was 15, his arm was mangled in the sawmill where he was working. He later hired out to work on the wharves of Richmond, where he befriended a sailor from Boston who helped him escape.

He found a series of odd jobs in Boston to support himself. Burns worked in a Brattle Street clothing store when his' owner discovered where he lived in Boston. Authorities identified him by a scar on his face that looked like a brand and an inch of bone protruding from his wrist.

The arrest horrified Wendell Phillips, the wealthy, 42-year-old son of Boston's first mayor, and the rest of the city's abolitionists. It wasn't so much that the Fugitive Slave Act was being enforced — it had taken effect in 1850. Burns' arrest came on the heels of the passage of the Kansas-Nebraska Act two days earlier. Kansas would certainly enter the Union as a slave state, and slavery opponents feared slavery could then seep north into Boston as well.

Indignation at Burns' arrest intensified because of the presence of several abolitionist and women's rights groups checking into Boston hotels for their annual convention.

The next day Wendell Phillips went to see the terrified Anthony Burns in the courthouse. He then persuaded him to accept legal help from Richard Henry Dana, Jr.

A large and furious crowd gathered at Faneuil Hall to protest Burns' capture. Phillips gave a speech, asking 500 volunteers to surround the courthouse the next day.

Unknown to him, another abolitionist, Thomas Wentworth Higginson, had bought axes and planned to attack the courthouse to free Burns that night. At a pre-arranged signal, the crowd surged toward the courthouse.

The Boston slave riot failed to free the prisoner, but killed a guard in the melee.

As many as a thousand troops poured into the city to restore order as the trial got under way.

After a four-day trial, the judge ordered Burns back to slavery as Phillips watched helplessly in the courtroom. He visited Burns in his cell. "Mr. Phillips," Burns implored, "has everything been done for me that can be done? Must I go back?"

Phillips replied, "Burns, there isn't humanity, there isn't justice enough here to save you; you must go back."

Richard Henry Dana, Jr., had pleaded in the courtroom for Burns' freedom for 4-1/2 hours. For his efforts he was attacked by pro-slavery rioters.

On June 2, the governor placed Boston under martial law. Anthony Burns was to be shipped back to Virginia. As guards prepared to march him to the ship, nearly 50,000 people lined the streets, held back by Marines and police officers. Storefronts were draped in black, and people hung out upper windows spitting on the soldiers as the crowd shrieked, 'Shame! Shame!' Burns walked through the crowd with his head held high to the ship that would carry him back to Virginia.

Boston would long remember the sight of a solitary black man walking through a gauntlet of federal troops holding back crowds. President Franklin Pierce had hoped that stern enforcement of the Fugitive Slave Law would quell opposition to it. But he miscalculated badly. The Boston slave riot intensified feelings against slavery in Massachusetts as the federal troops had seemed to place the commonwealth "under the feet of Virginia."

Wendell Phillips sank into depression, from which he emerged with fresh resolve to take his anti-slavery message out of Boston to the Ohio Valley and the Great Lakes. He had the blessing of his invalid wife, who would spend long weeks at home without him.

Burns wrote to Phillips from a jail in Richmond, Va., asking him to "dow all you can for me." His owner refused to sell him to abolitionists, who had raised $1,200 for the purchase.

Finally, Anthony Burns was put on the auction block and sold to David McDaniel. McDaniel did agree to sell Burns to the Boston abolitionists for $1,300. He then returned to Boston.

Wendell Phillips arranged for Anthony Burns to attend Oberlin College, where an anonymous donor gave him a scholarship. Anthony Burns would graduate, become a Baptist minister, and die of tuberculosis at the age of 28.[1]

The case of Anthony Burns is just one example of the escaped slaves who were captured. There are a plethora of others that were treated similarly or worse.

At least with him, he was eventually freed, before Lincoln's Emancipation Proclamation, and he was able to have success in his life, although unfortunately that too was cut short due to his early death.

Many others that were wrongfully convicted never got to taste their freedom until after the Civil War.

If nothing else, the case of Anthony Burns, and the subsequent Boston riots, enlightened a lot Americans who were unaware of the egregious situation.

This also aided the abolition movement, while simultaneously angering the slave owners and pro slavery Southerners.

The Boston Riots were only the beginning.

THE REPUBLICAN PARTY: FORMED IN 1854 TO END SLAVER...

CHAPTER THREE

The aftermath of Pierce's strict enforcement of the hideous Fugitive Slave Act, in addition to the newly introduced Kansas-Nebraska Act, and it's imminent passage, sent the tensions over the edge.

A large part of this country had seen enough and yearned for a change of direction.

That's when that brave group of former members of the Whig Party, and anti-slavery Democrats got together to form the Republican Party on that monumental day, at a schoolhouse in Ripon, Wisconsin.

Prior to that day, where the name "Republican" was first used, on February 24, 1854, this group of people had informally met, also in Ripon, Wisconsin to talk about their displeasure of this soon to be law.

On May 30th, 1854 the Kansas-Nebraska Act bill was officially signed into law by President Pierce.

The new upstart party knew that they had no time to waste, and that action had to be done to finally stop the Southern Democrats and their vile ways.

Several months after their first unofficial meeting, the very first statewide convention under the new Republican party was held near Jackson, Michigan.

Oddly enough, it was held on July 6th, 1854, just two days after the anniversary of this great country's freedom from England.

By now this movement had quickly grown as this first organized meeting of the Republican Party had an estimated 10,000 people attend.

"The Constitution Center" website noted that newspaper publisher, Horace Greeley, not only made the name official, but had this to say in an editorial before that historic meeting,

'"We should not care much whether those thus united [against slavery] were designated 'Whig,' 'Free Democrat' or something else; though we think some simple name like 'Republican' would more fitly designate those who had united to restore the Union to its true mission of champion and promulgator of Liberty rather than propagandist of slavery," he wrote.'

The website added,

'Today, the official Republican Party website

recognizes that the party's first meeting was held in Ripon, and that "the Party was formally organized in July 1854 by thousands of anti-slavery activists at a convention in Jackson, Michigan." (There is still some disagreement, at least in Michigan and Wisconsin, about bragging rights.)'

It was a beginning for this new, anti-slavery party, and they new that it would take a lot of work, as well as navigating through the heightened tensions thanks to President Pierce and the Southern Democrats.

At that time, this new party was mostly concentrated in the Midwest, which makes sense since it was the Kansas-Nebraska Act that was the final straw.

They had some interest in other anti-slavery states, but zero in the Southern slave owning states.

In their first elections in 1854, there were some positive results as they were able to get their candidate, Kinsley Bingham, across the finish line to become the new Governor of Michigan.

They had some initial competition in the Northern States by a group known as the Know Nothings. But that group was much divided and a couple of years later was pretty much gone.

Despite some early progress, the newly formed Republican Party knew that there was a lot of work to be done.

Not only wouldn't it be easy, but it would dangerous as well.

One example of this was as a result of the Kansas-Nebraska Act that would become known as "Bleeding Kansas".

Some consider this short period of time, from 1854-1859, as the unofficial start to the Civil War as it was fought between the proslavery and antislavery groups for control of Kansas.

Britannica.com states,

'Sponsors of the Kansas-Nebraska Act (May 30, 1854) expected its provisions for territorial self-government to arrest the "torrent of fanaticism" that had been dividing the nation regarding the slavery issue. Instead, free-soil forces from the North formed armed emigrant associations to populate Kansas, while proslavery advocates poured over the border from Missouri. Regulating associations and guerrilla bands were formed by each side, and only the intervention of the governor prevented violence in the Wakarusa War, launched in December 1855 over the murder of an antislavery settler.

"Bleeding Kansas" became a fact with the Sack of Lawrence (May 21, 1856), in which a proslavery mob swarmed into the town of Lawrence and wrecked and burned the hotel and newspaper office in an effort to wipe out the "hotbed of abolitionism." The day after the attack on Lawrence, the conflict spread to the floor of the U.S. Senate, where U.S. Sen. Charles Sumner of Massachusetts was viciously beaten with a cane by U.S. Rep. Preston S. Brooks of South Carolina in response to Sumner's impassioned address regarding the "Crime Against Kansas" committed by supporters of slavery.

Three days after the Sack of Lawrence, an antislavery band led by John Brown retaliated in the Pottawatomie Massacre. After the attack Brown's name evoked fear and rage in slavery apologists in Kansas. Periodic bloodshed along the border followed as the two factions fought battles, captured towns, and set prisoners free.

A political struggle to determine the future state's position on slavery ensued, centered on the Lecompton Constitution proposed in 1857. The question was finally settled when Kansas was admitted as a free state in January 1861, but, meanwhile, "Bleeding Kansas" had furnished the newly formed Republican Party with a much needed antislavery issue in the national election of 1860. Claims for $400,000 in damages sustained in the border war were later approved by territorial commissioners.[1]

Before the end of "Bleeding Kansas", the newly formed, Republican Party, was still working on gaining more support prior to the election of 1856.

Although they had made great strides with their movement, their Presidential candidate John C.

Fremont, lost the 1856 election to Democrat, James Buchanan.

Buchanan had easily defeated the incumbent President, Franklin Pierce in the primary.

Pierce was an unmitigated disaster as President, whose policies and rhetoric sent this country on a one way path towards the Civil War.

Whatever slim chances of avoiding a civil war quickly evaporated when Buchanan, in his victory speech labeled Republicans as "dangerous" as well as stating emphatically that they had wrongly attacked the Southern states.

His solution to the Kansas-Nebraska Act was what was known as "popular sovereignty", which in this case basically meant that the states themselves would have control over the situation and not the federal government.

By doing this, he essentially told the states involved that if they wanted slavery to continue, then so be it.

He also was out to destroy the upstart Republican Party.

This, of course, was basically just an extension of President Pierce's actions which only heightened the Republicans' resolve.

THOMAS YOUNG

CHAPTER FOUR

As the violence and tensions persisted through Buchanan's reign as President, the Republican Party and the abolition movement as a whole, was growing stronger.

This was never more evident than in the election of 1860, when the Republican Party nominated Abraham Lincoln.

Prior to becoming a Republican, Lincoln was part of the waning, Whig Party.

In 1856 he left the Whig Party and joined the Republican Party. He was extremely anti-slavery and back when he was a Whig he was extremely opposed to the Kansas-Nebraska Act. He vehemently spoke out against it, as well as about the spreading of slavery, and added, "I hate it because of the monstrous injustice of slavery itself".

In 1856 when he joined the Republican Party, he was brought against the very powerful Democrat, Senator Stephen Douglas.

After a confrontation with Douglas, things skyrocketed for Lincoln.

History.com writes,

'Events conspired to push him back into national politics, however: Douglas, a leading Democrat in Congress, had pushed through the passage of the Kansas-Nebraska Act (1854), which declared that the voters of each territory, rather than the federal government, had the right to decide whether the territory should be slave or free.

On October 16, 1854, Lincoln went before a large crowd in Peoria to debate the merits of the Kansas-Nebraska Act with Douglas, denouncing slavery and its extension and calling the institution a violation of the most basic tenets of the Declaration of Independence.

With the Whig Party in ruins, Lincoln joined the new Republican Party–formed largely in opposition to slavery's extension into the territories–in 1856 and ran for the Senate again that year (he had campaigned unsuccessfully for the seat in 1855 as well). In June, Lincoln delivered his now-famous "house divided" speech, in which he quoted from the Gospels to illustrate his belief that "this government cannot endure, permanently, half slave and half free."

Lincoln then squared off against Douglas in a series of famous debates; though he lost the Senate election, Lincoln's performance made his reputation nationally.

Abraham Lincoln's 1860 Presidential Campaign

Lincoln's profile rose even higher in early 1860 after he delivered another rousing speech at New York City's Cooper Union. That May, Republicans chose Lincoln as their candidate for president, passing over Senator William H. Seward of New York and other powerful contenders in favor of the rangy Illinois lawyer with only one undistinguished congressional term under his belt.

In the general election, Lincoln again faced Douglas, who represented the northern Democrats; southern Democrats had nominated John C. Breckenridge of Kentucky, while John Bell ran for the brand new Constitutional Union Party. With Breckenridge and Bell splitting the vote in the South, Lincoln won most of the North and carried the Electoral College to win the White House.

He built an exceptionally strong cabinet composed of many of his political rivals, including Seward, Salmon P. Chase, Edward Bates and Edwin M. Stanton.'

The Republicans knew that they had their man, but they also knew that things were about to explode in this country.

Soon after this election, the Civil War began on April 12th, 1961, as Confederate troops attacked Fort Sumter and the Union troops.

The war continued on, until it finally ended, nearly 4 years later, on April 9th, 1965.

It took its toll, however, on both the North and the South as over 600,000 soldiers were killed and millions more were injured.

The South was nearly completely demolished in many areas as the North became victorious in this bloodbath.

One of the main positive results that came from the war was that during the Civil War, Republican President, Abraham Lincoln signed the Emancipation Proclamation which gave the slaves in this country their freedom.

From the National Archives, here is the official transcript of the historic document that the very brave, President Lincoln, signed,

'Transcript of the Proclamation

January 1, 1863

A Transcription

By the President of the United States of America:

A Proclamation.

Whereas, on the twenty-second day of September, in the year of our Lord one thousand eight hundred and sixty-two, a proclamation was issued by the President of the United States, containing, among other things, the following, to wit:

"That on the first day of January, in the year of our Lord one thousand eight hundred and sixty-three, all persons held as slaves within any State or designated part of a State, the people whereof shall then be in rebellion against the United States, shall be then, thenceforward, and forever free; and the Executive Government of the United States, including the military and naval authority thereof, will recognize and maintain the freedom of such persons, and will do no act or acts to repress such persons, or any of them, in any efforts they may make for their actual freedom.

"That the Executive will, on the first day of January aforesaid, by proclamation, designate the States and parts of States, if any, in which the people thereof, respectively, shall then be in rebellion against the United States; and the fact that any State, or the people thereof, shall on that day be, in good faith, represented in the Congress of the United States by members chosen thereto at elections wherein a majority of the qualified voters of such State shall have participated, shall, in the absence of strong countervailing testimony, be deemed conclusive evidence that such State, and the people thereof, are not then in rebellion against the United States."

Now, therefore I, Abraham Lincoln, President of the United States, by virtue of the power in me vested as Commander-in-Chief, of the Army and Navy of the United States in time of actual armed rebellion against the authority and government of the United States, and as a fit and necessary war measure for suppressing said rebellion, do, on this first day of January, in the year of our Lord one thousand eight hundred and sixty-three, and in accordance with my purpose so to do publicly proclaimed for the full period of one hundred days, from the day first above mentioned, order and designate as the States and parts of States wherein the people thereof respectively, are this day in rebellion against the United States, the following, to wit:

Arkansas, Texas, Louisiana, (except the Parishes of St. Bernard, Plaquemines, Jefferson, St. John, St. Charles, St. James Ascension, Assumption, Terrebonne, Lafourche, St. Mary, St. Martin, and Orleans, including the City of New Orleans) Mississippi, Alabama, Florida, Georgia, South Carolina, North Carolina, and Virginia, (except the forty-eight counties designated as West Virginia, and also the counties of Berkley, Accomac, Northampton, Elizabeth City, York, Princess Ann, and Norfolk, including the cities of Norfolk and Portsmouth[)], and which excepted parts, are for the present, left precisely as if this proclamation were not issued.

And by virtue of the power, and for the purpose aforesaid, I do order and declare that all persons held as slaves within said designated States, and parts of States, are, and henceforward shall be free; and that the Executive government of the United States, including the military and naval authorities thereof, will recognize and maintain the freedom of said persons.

And I hereby enjoin upon the people so declared to be free to abstain from all violence, unless in necessary self-defence; and I recommend to them that, in all cases when allowed, they labor faithfully for reasonable wages.

And I further declare and make known, that such persons of suitable condition, will be received into the armed service of the United States to garrison forts, positions, stations, and other places, and to man vessels of all sorts in said service.

And upon this act, sincerely believed to be an

act of justice, warranted by the Constitution, upon military necessity, I invoke the considerate judgment of mankind, and the gracious favor of Almighty God.

In witness whereof, I have hereunto set my hand and caused the seal of the United States to be affixed.

Done at the City of Washington, this first day of January, in the year of our Lord one thousand eight hundred and sixty three, and of the Independence of the United States of America the eighty-seventh.

By the President: ABRAHAM LINCOLN

WILLIAM H. SEWARD, Secretary of State.'

THE REPUBLICAN PARTY: FORMED IN 1854 TO END SLAVER...

CHAPTER FIVE

Following this, was one of the biggest amendments ever to the US Constitution, the 13th Amendment.

The Thirteenth Amendment officially abolished slavery and involuntary servitude.

It was passed by the Senate on April 8, 1864, by the House of Representatives on January 31, 1865, and by the end of 1865 (December 6, 1865), it was ratified by Georgia which became the required 27th of the 36 states that existed back then, to fulfill the requirement, that 3 quarters of the states approve of an amendment to the US Constitution.

Although he was there for the beginning, unfortunately President Lincoln wasn't around for the final passage of the law.

These were monumentally historic moments for

this country, but they were not in Lincoln's personal best interest as his bravery in his fight to free the wrongfully enslaved people in this country, and to help black men, women and children in this country, would lead to his assassination.

Just days after the end of the Civil War, on April 14th 1865, President Abraham Lincoln was shot and killed while watching a performance of "Our American Cousin" at Ford's Theatre in Washington D.C., by John Wilkes Booth, a Confederate sympathizer.

At 7:22 a.m., the next morning, on April 15th, Lincoln was pronounced dead from the gunshot injury to the left side of his head.

Shortly after a brief mourning period, things would drastically change when Andrew Johnson, his vice President, and a Democrat took over as President.

A true wolf in sheep's clothing, Johnson was in favor of the Southern states rejoining the United States, but without the recently freed slaves having any of the protections that they were supposed to have by law.

This led to his impeachment, though he had enough Democrats in the Senate that supported him to allow him to be acquitted in the Senate by just one vote.

Prior to this, he presided over what was known as the Reconstruction Era.

Britannica.com gives a detailed explanation of the Reconstruction Era which reads,

'The national debate over Reconstruction began during the Civil War. In December 1863, less than a year after he issued the Emancipation Proclamation, Pres. Abraham Lincoln announced the first comprehensive program for Reconstruction, the Ten Percent Plan. Under it, when one-tenth of a state's prewar voters took an oath of loyalty, they could establish a new state government. To Lincoln, the plan was an attempt to weaken the Confederacy rather than a blueprint for the postwar South. It was put into operation in parts of the Union-occupied Confederacy, but none of the new governments achieved broad local support. In 1864 Congress enacted (and Lincoln pocket vetoed) the Wade-Davis Bill, which proposed to delay the formation of new Southern governments until a majority of voters had taken a loyalty oath. Some Republicans were already convinced that equal rights for the former slaves had to accompany the South's readmission to the Union. In his last speech, on April 11, 1865, Lincoln, referring to Reconstruction in Louisiana, expressed the view that some Blacks—the "very intelligent" and those who had served in the Union army—ought to enjoy the right to vote.

Following Lincoln's assassination in April 1865, Andrew Johnson became president and inaugurated the period of Presidential Reconstruction (1865–

67). Johnson offered a pardon to all Southern whites except Confederate leaders and wealthy planters (although most of these subsequently received individual pardons), restoring their political rights and all property except slaves. He also outlined how new state governments would be created. Apart from the requirement that they abolish slavery, repudiate secession, and abrogate the Confederate debt, these governments were granted a free hand in managing their affairs. They responded by enacting the Black codes, laws that required African Americans to sign yearly labour contracts and in other ways sought to limit the freedmen's economic options and reestablish plantation discipline. African Americans strongly resisted the implementation of these measures, and they seriously undermined Northern support for Johnson's policies.

When Congress assembled in December 1865, Radical Republicans such as Rep. Thaddeus Stevens of Pennsylvania and Sen. Charles Sumner from Massachusetts called for the establishment of new Southern governments based on equality before the law and universal male suffrage. But the more numerous moderate Republicans hoped to work with Johnson while modifying his program. Congress refused to seat the representatives and senators elected from the Southern states and in early 1866 passed the Freedmen's Bureau and Civil

Rights Bills. The first extended the life of an agency Congress had created in 1865 to oversee the transition from slavery to freedom. The second defined all persons born in the United States as national citizens, who were to enjoy equality before the law.

A combination of personal stubbornness, fervent belief in states' rights, and racist convictions led Johnson to reject these bills, causing a permanent rupture between himself and Congress. The Civil Rights Act became the first significant legislation in American history to become law over a president's veto. Shortly thereafter, Congress approved the Fourteenth Amendment, which put the principle of birthright citizenship into the Constitution and forbade states to deprive any citizen of the "equal protection" of the laws. Arguably the most important addition to the Constitution other than the Bill of Rights, the amendment constituted a profound change in federal-state relations. Traditionally, citizens' rights had been delineated and protected by the states. Thereafter, the federal government would guarantee all Americans' equality before the law against state violation.

In the fall 1866 congressional elections, Northern voters overwhelmingly repudiated Johnson's policies. Congress decided to begin Reconstruction anew. The Reconstruction Acts of 1867 divided the South into five military districts and outlined how new governments, based on manhood suffrage without regard to race, were to be established. Thus began the period of Radical or Congressional Reconstruction, which lasted until the end of the last Southern Republican governments in 1877.

By 1870 all the former Confederate states had been readmitted to the Union, and nearly all were controlled by the Republican Party. Three groups made up Southern Republicanism. Carpetbaggers, or recent arrivals from the North, were former Union soldiers, teachers, Freedmen's Bureau agents, and businessmen. The second large group, scalawags, or native-born white Republicans, included some businessmen and planters, but most were non slaveholding small farmers from the Southern up-country. Loyal to the Union during the Civil War, they saw the Republican Party as a means of keeping Confederates from regaining power in the South.

In every state, African Americans formed the overwhelming majority of Southern Republican voters. From the beginning of Reconstruction, Black conventions and newspapers throughout the South had called for the extension of full civil and political rights to African Americans. Composed of those who had been free before the Civil War plus slave ministers, artisans, and Civil War veterans, the Black political leadership pressed for the elimination of the racial caste system and the economic uplifting of the former slaves. Sixteen African Americans served in Congress during Reconstruction—including Hiram Revels and Blanche K. Bruce in the U.S. Senate —more than 600 in state legislatures, and hundreds more in local offices from sheriff to justice of the peace scattered across the South. So-called "Black supremacy" never existed, but the advent of African Americans in positions of political power marked a dramatic break with the country's traditions and aroused bitter hostility from Reconstruction's opponents.

Serving an expanded citizenry, Reconstruction governments established the South's first state-funded public school systems, sought to strengthen the bargaining power of plantation labourers, made taxation more equitable, and outlawed racial discrimination in public transportation and accommodations. They also offered lavish aid to railroads and other enterprises in the hope of creating a "New South" whose economic expansion would benefit Blacks and whites alike. But the economic program spawned corruption and rising taxes, alienating increasing numbers of white voters.

Meanwhile, the social and economic transformation of the South proceeded apace. To Blacks, freedom meant independence from white control. Reconstruction provided the opportunity for African Americans to solidify their family ties and to create independent religious institutions, which became centers of community life that survived long after Reconstruction ended. The former slaves also demanded economic independence. Blacks' hopes that the federal government would provide them with land had been raised by Gen. William T. Sherman's Field Order No. 15 of January 1865, which set aside a large swath of land along the coast of South Carolina and Georgia for the exclusive settlement of Black families, and by the Freedmen's Bureau Act of March, which authorized the bureau to rent or sell land in its possession to former slaves. But President Johnson in the summer of 1865 ordered land in federal hands to be returned to its former owners. The dream of "40 acres and a mule" was stillborn. Lacking land, most former slaves had little economic alternative other than resuming work on plantations owned by whites. Some worked for wages, others as sharecroppers, who divided the crop with the owner at the end of the year. Neither status offered much hope for economic mobility. For decades, most Southern Blacks remained propertyless and poor.

Nonetheless, the political revolution of Reconstruction spawned increasingly violent opposition from white Southerners. White supremacist organizations that committed terrorist acts, such as the Ku Klux Klan, targeted local Republican leaders for beatings or assassination. African Americans who asserted their rights in dealings with white employers, teachers, ministers, and others seeking to assist the former slaves also became targets. At Colfax, Louisiana, in 1873, scores of Black militiamen were killed after surrendering to armed whites intent on seizing control of local government. Increasingly, the new Southern governments looked to Washington, D.C., for assistance.

By 1869 the Republican Party was firmly in control of all three branches of the federal government. After attempting to remove Secretary of War Edwin M. Stanton, in violation of the new Tenure of Office Act, Johnson had been impeached by the House of Representatives in 1868. Although the Senate, by a single vote, failed to remove him from office, Johnson's power to obstruct the course of Reconstruction was gone. Republican Ulysses S. Grant was elected president that fall (see United States presidential election of 1868). Soon afterward, Congress approved the Fifteenth Amendment, prohibiting states from restricting the right to vote because of race. Then it enacted a series of Enforcement Acts authorizing national action to suppress political violence. In 1871 the administration launched a legal and military offensive that destroyed the Klan. Grant was reelected in 1872 in the most peaceful election of the period.'

The Democrats, during and after the Reconstruction Era, tried everything they could to keep black people in this country down.

The Britannica article mentioned "The Black Codes" and the "Ku Klux Klan". In addition to this there were other obstacles, such as "Jim Crow laws".

The latter two remained a part of many racist Democrats way of thinking for decades to come.

All three were designed and implemented by the hateful, racist Democrats, to stop Black Americans from being able to prosper in any way possible.

The Black Codes led into the infamous, "Jim Crow laws. "

Battlefield.org paints a descriptive picture of this, as they said,

'The Emancipation Proclamation took effect on January 1, 1863, granting freedom to all enslaved people within rebelling territories. In January 1865, General William T. Sherman issued Special Field Orders No. 15, reserving confiscated land on the coast of Georgia and South Carolina for the use of freedpeople, each family to be given 40 acres, which was the source for the expression "forty acres and a mule." The same month, the

Thirteenth Amendment was passed by Congress, officially abolishing the institution of slavery in the United States. President Abraham Lincoln had hinted towards granting suffrage to black males. As clean cut as this sounds, the situation for formerly enslaved people on the ground was much more complicated. Their lives had been changed dramatically in a short amount of time, and some of them had nothing but the clothes on their back. While initially celebrating emancipation and the end of the war, many freedpeople were now wondering, "Now what?"

In March 1865, the Bureau of Refugees, Freedmen, and Abandoned Lands, or the Freedmen's Bureau, was established to assist these newly freed people. The bureau helped African Americans find family members from whom they were separated during the war, gave them necessary food and medical aid, established schools throughout the South, and helped them secure fair employment. However, its efficacy was soon under attack by Southern state governments.

Lincoln was assassinated on April 15, and now the task of Reconstruction fell to his vice president—now president—Andrew Johnson. However, Johnson had a very different vision of what Reconstruction should look like than his predecessor. The Tennessee native favored leniency to former Confederates, granting them full amnesty, allowing them to once again become full citizens. Johnson also rescinded Sherman's "forty acres and a mule" order, returning the land to its former owners, regardless of the blacks who had already settled there. Only whites could vote for delegates to and participate in the conventions, and they were often dominated by ex-Confederates who wanted to restore the status quo from before the war. As a result, blacks had no voice in their states' governments. Because a condition of rejoining the Union was ratifying the Thirteenth Amendment, slavery in its former form could not be implemented. Instead, Southern governments began to write black codes to restrict the freedom of formerly enslaved people and guarantee the continuation of a cheap labor force. They were a perpetuation of antebellum slave codes, although they granted limited civil rights, such as being able to make contracts and marry.

The most infamous of these black codes were from Mississippi and South Carolina, although nearly every Southern state enacted some sort of black code. Mississippi propagated slavery in a different form by forcing blacks to have written evidence of employment at the start of each year. If they failed to do so, they could forfeit their wages or be arrested. South Carolina's black code prohibited blacks from having an occupation outside of agriculture or domestic work unless they paid an annual tax, which hit urban blacks especially hard. Punishments in both these states also included "hiring out" the perpetrator to do free labor.

Northerners were enraged by what they saw as Southerners completely ignoring the results of the war. As a result, Congress passed the Civil Rights Act of 1866, a bill that had been introduced in 1865 but was vetoed by Johnson. He vetoed it again in 1866, but this time, both chambers overrode the veto – the first time Congress ever overrode the president's veto of major legislation. The act was intended to protect the civil rights of blacks, which were being trampled upon by Southern state governments. But some in Congress believed that Congress didn't have the power to enact the legislation. Thus, it wasn't until 1868 when the Fourteenth Amendment was passed that the Civil Rights Act became law.'

This Amendment stopped the black codes as it said that anyone who was born in the United States was a citizen and that meant they were all subject to equal protection.

This led to Black Americans being elected into office in Southern states for the first time ever. Unfortunately though, this good turn around had plenty of obstacles from the racist Democrats.

The same Battlefield.org story stated,

'For a time, it seemed as if this new status quo of equality for all would persist in the South. Blacks had a large role in rewriting state constitutions and participated in public life in unprecedented numbers. The Ku Klux Klan, after its initial reign of terror in 1867-69, was essentially destroyed by Ulysses S. Grant, his newly created Department of Justice, and the U.S. army.

However, Northern support for Reconstruction waned, and after the election of President Rutherford B. Hayes, Reconstruction was at an end as the military withdrew and once again left the South to its own devices. The coming years would see the emergence of Jim Crow laws, which sought to undermine African Americans' voting and civil rights as another perpetuation of the black codes.'

As mentioned, the Ku Klux Klan also emerged around the Reconstruction Era. This hideous group was founded by the racist sore losers of the Civil War.

Among the original members who formed the KKK in Pulaski, Tennessee, in 1865 were Confederate soldiers who had survived the war.

By 1867, they had begun to spread (like roaches) to the point where they had their own conventions, and had started what they called an "Invisible

Empire of the South."

This organization became more powerful and dangerous as they became more structured with Nathan Bedford Forrest becoming their first Grand Wizard.

Underneath him they created other positions of power within their organization such as grand dragons, grand titans and exulted cyclops.

Their hatred of blacks was evident in not only their repulsive rhetoric, but also in their heinous actions.

By 1870, the south was becoming more infested with the KKK as they were in nearly every southern state.

Of course these cowards dressed in their white hoods and robes to hide their identity.

One question that I've always wondered, "If they were so proud of what they were doing, then why did they need the hoods to cover their faces?"

Their abhorrent rhetoric and actions had no boundaries. There are far too many examples of this, but one that sticks out occurred back in 1871 when around 500 of these cowards attacked a jail in South Carolina and ruthlessly lynched and murdered 8 black prisoners.

500 on 8, that's a real fair fight. But that's how these despicable cowards operated.

Thanks to the racist Democrats, heinous events, including lynchings, would become a staple for these animals for years and decades to come.

In addition to the Black Codes and the formation of the KKK, the racist Southern Democrats still had another trick up their slimy sleeves.

Even though the passage of the 13th amendment have black people in this country their freedom, the Southern Democrats just after the Civil War were able to do an end run around that law when they created what was known as Jim Crow laws.

These were laws that began in the Southern states that legalized segregation based on race.

Black Americans in certain southern areas were denied their right to vote, get any type of education or even find employment.

The despicable Democrats were able to spread their vile hatred against Black Americans in communities throughout the country.

Their repulsive contempt for Black Americans resulted in segregation everywhere from restrooms to hospitals to elevators to entrances of buildings to even cemeteries.

More examples of the forced segregation instituted by the hateful Democrats was seemingly endless.

There were even neighborhoods where Black Americans weren't even allowed to live.

The racist Democrats unfortunately worked their disgusting Jim Crow laws in more and more areas throughout the country.

However, thanks to the Republicans continuing to fight for Black Americans, there were still many parts of the country that was free of the horrific tyranny.

In these areas, Black Americans could live free, like they were supposed to without fear as opposed to those Black Americans who lived in municipalities where Jim Crow laws thrived.

Those who lived there risked it all including everything from jail time to death if they dared defy the powerful Democrat racists who ran things.

The Republicans did their best to stop this tyranny against the "Freedmen", as many of the Black Americans were referred to as they had legally, by the Emancipation Proclamation, to become free people.

Eventually the power that the Democratic leaders had began to fade away and in 1964 after the passage of the Civil Rights Act, Jim Crow laws were once and for all exterminated.

Unfortunately though there were still many obstacles to overcome to get to that point.

By the end of the 1800's, both of the Democrats schemes against Black Americans were in full swing.

THE REPUBLICAN PARTY: FORMED IN 1854 TO END SLAVER...

CHAPTER SIX

Going into the 1900s, the treatment of black Americans didn't get any better with Jim Crow laws in full swing, the KKK worse than ever, and then came the election of the most racist President of the 20th century, Woodrow Wilson.

The abysmal treatment of black people in this country by many in the Democratic Party continued into the 1900's as their Jim Crow laws and the rise of their aforementioned KKK combined to inhibit the growth of many black Americans.

Fortunately, there were many that were able to overcome those obstacles, but there were still others that weren't able to do so.

The Republican Party continued its fight against the harshness and wouldn't let up in its battle to help black people in this country succeed, or at least have the chance to succeed.

The massive roadblocks put up by the racist Democrats continued to thwart progress as by the early 1900's it was virtually impossible for a black person in this country to hold public office.

This situation, as well as the treatment of Black people in general, wasn't helped with the election of Woodrow Wilson in 1912. He went onto hold the office of the Presidency from March 4, 1913 - March 4, 1921.

To say that he was a racist, is an understatement!

Along with his racist policies, he made sure that there were segregationists in his cabinet and was often an apologist for the Confederacy.

This racist Democrat even had the nerve to show a pro-KKK movie in the White House.

The movie, "The Birth of a Nation", was the first movie ever to be shown there.

After public outrage over the playing of this despicable movie, he, like most racist cowards, shriveled down and attempted to tell an obvious lie and said that he hadn't seen the movie prior to it being shown.

So we are supposed to believe that a man who had racist policies, a cabinet with segregationists, told racist jokes, was an apologist for the Confederacy, knew nothing of this odious message that was in this movie?

I think a "dog ate my homework" excuse is more

believable.

This would lead up to a very dark time in American history as just a few years after Wilson had left the White House, the Democrats put on the 1924 Democratic National Convention.

Many would go on to refer to it as the "Klanbake".

It was given that name due to the heavy KKK presence at the convention as well as a KKK favorite as a Democratic candidate for the Presidency.

Politico had an in-depth story on this abysmal mark in history and said,

'The convention is often called the "Klanbake" because one of the front-runners, white shoe lawyer and former Wilson Cabinet member William G. McAdoo, was supported by the Ku Klux Klan. The Klan was a major source of power within the party, and McAdoo did not repudiate its endorsement. The other front-runner, New York Governor Al Smith, a Catholic who represented the party's anti-Klan, anti-Prohibition wing (McAdoo also backed Prohibition, which was then the law of the land), and his faction failed by a slim margin to pass a platform plank condemning the Klan. The convention, which was held in Madison Square Garden, had no black delegates.

As a two-thirds vote was needed to win the nomination, McAdoo and Smith essentially canceled each other out and the scores of "favorite sons" placed into nomination prevented either man from collecting even a simple majority of votes. A total of 19 candidates got votes on the first ballot. By the time the thing concluded, 60 different candidates had received a delegate's vote. Floor demonstrations abounded between ballots, with the chants for "Mac! Mac! McAdoo!" countered by Smith's forces who cried out, "Ku, Ku, McAdoo," as Robert K. Murray writes in his splendid 1976 book The 103rd Ballot. Fistfights and screaming matches, featuring choice obscenities were common. On Independence Day, the 10th day of the convention, 20,000 Klansmen amassed across the Hudson River in New Jersey to burn crosses and punish effigies of Smith.'

Through the heated mess neither Smith nor McAdoo would get enough votes.

Despite dozens and dozens of ballots, the Democrats couldn't get enough votes to upend the racist, KKK candidate.

Politico added,

'When the debris began to fall, somebody looked underneath the pile and dragged out John W. Davis," wrote New York Times reporter Arthur C. Krock. The 1924 convention wasn't the Democratic Party's first experiment in conventional chaos. The 1912 convention took 46 ballots to select Woodrow Wilson, and the 1920 convention spent 44 ballots on picking James Cox. But the 1924 convention appears to have wounded the Democratic Party, which failed spectacularly in the fall election. Davis collected only 28.8 percent of the vote against the winner, Republican President Calvin Coolidge (54 percent), and third-place finisher Progressive Party candidate Robert M. La Follette Sr. (16.6 percent).'

This was a dark stain on the fabric of this country and even though 2024 is the 100th anniversary of this event, there's barely a blip about this on today's mainstream media's radar.

They try their best to cover up the Democrats long history of anti-black actions and rhetoric.

The 1920s were a time when the KKK and Jim Crow laws were at their peak. Even when they may have begun to slip, these factions were still very powerful.

By the 1940's both the Jim Crow laws and the KKK were going strong when a soon to be force on the Democratic scene was emerging.

This man was Robert Byrd, who would go on to be the longest serving Senator in US history.

Byrd became the face of the Democrats for decades, from the 1950s through his death in 2010.

Although there have been racists on both sides that have tried to keep black people in this country down, the overwhelming majority has come from one side, the Democrats, while the other side, the Republicans have continually tried to thwart their efforts.

The man at the forefront of the Democrats, throughout the mid to late 1900s, in this attempt was none other than Robert Byrd.

Democratic Senator, Robert Byrd would go on to lead an unscrupulous life that has been whitewashed by many in the mainstream media, fellow Democrats, so-called activists and others for ideological, political, economic or other reasons, as well as those who occupy themselves with the willful blindness school of thought.

They tend to glaze over decades of his hateful, racist, demeaning actions and rhetoric to focus on the small amount of good that he did. They accept his continued faux apologies as if they were gospel.

Later, they will be further called out for their own covering up for such an insidious human being.

Byrd somehow became the record holder as a Senator when he was elected to the US Senate on November 7, 2006 for a ninth full term.

Prior to that he was a US congressman, beginning with his first national political victory in 1952.

Even more astounding, with all of his history, is that on November 18, 2009 Byrd became the longest serving member in the centuries of this great nation at 20,996 days.

Long before he served in Congress (as a Congressman, then as a Senator), Byrd organized his own chapter of the KKK in the 1942. Not only did he organize his own chapter, he became a KKK leader as he recruited over 150 other racist scumbags. He was not only considered a leader, but one of the KKK's top people at the time, rising to the level of Exalted Cyclops.

Back in the 1940's, everyone knew not only what the KKK was, but also despicable they were. After all, the reason that they all wore hoods was that they didn't want anyone to recognize them.

After over a year as a KKK leader, he left the organization and followed the advice of those in the KKK who called him a born leader and pursued a career in politics. He started at the state level and won a seat in the West Virginia House of Delegates in 1946, where represented Raleigh County from 1947 to 1950. It was at that point where he began his political journey on a federal level and was elected into the U.S. House of Representatives in 1952 and served there until he ran for Senate, and won, in 1958.

Along this journey he continually apologized for his time in the KKK. He made it appear that being in the KKK was a little mistake that he made.

He tried to play down the racism part, despite rising to the level of Exalted Cyclops and recruiting over 150 other racist dirt bags.

Despite his later claims about why he joined the KKK and that it wasn't because of racism, letters that he had written from early on strongly refute any iota of a doubt as to why he joined the KKK, and even after he left, how strong those repulsive feelings flowed through every vein in his body.

One such letter was one that in 1945, well after he left the KKK, he wrote to then Senator Theodore Bilbo, of Mississippi (who happened to be a segregationist U.S. Senator).

Byrd was furious over President Harry Truman's efforts to integrate the U.S. military.

He did not mince words as he wrote,

"I shall never fight in the armed forces with a Negro by my side… Rather I should die a thousand times, and see Old Glory trampled in the dirt never to rise again, than to see this beloved land of ours become degraded by race mongrels, a throwback to the blackest specimen from the wilds."

How anyone could possibly elect someone into either state, or federal government positions, after reading that letter that showed the true ugliness of his heart, is beyond me.

As bad as this was, for Robert Byrd, this was only the beginning.

A couple of years later, the hatred of black people continued to flow through his veins as in 1947, as a member of the Virginia House of Delegates, he wrote a letter to the Grand Wizard of the KKK where he said,

"The Klan is needed today as never before and I am anxious to see its rebirth here in West Virginia and in every state in the nation."

Even though he left the KKK so that he could pursue a career in politics, everything that they stood for was obviously still entrenched deep in his soul.

By the 1940's, the KKK was on a roll. By the 1920's they had surpassed an astounding 5 million members nationwide, with no signs of slowing down.

At the time that he joined, and recruited many more racists, then left, and still heavily supported them, the KKK was in full throttle with their spread of racial hatred.

There were far too many examples to show all of their heinous actions.

From his time as a leader of the KKK, to heavy recruiter, to years after, where he was a strong supporter of them and their actions as evidenced by not only his earlier actions but also his words that he spoke to such people as the racist Senator, Bilbo, as well as the Grand Wizard of the KKK, the KKK remained strong as their unscrupulous actions, which included lynchings, cross burnings the burning down of black churches and more were in full swing.

In fact, the cross burnings and burning down of black churches continued well into the 1960's.

In his 2005 memoir, he called the people in his KKK chapter, "outstanding people", as he claimed his chapter never committed any violence against black people.

He also inferred a claim that the KKK was a brief flirtation of his and he joined as a way of networking with people.

Although he denies not advocating, or committing, violence against black people (that can neither be definitively confirmed or denied), his disparaging, vile sentiments towards them can't be denied.

I'm sorry Mr. Byrd, but your actions and words contradict these assertions as your over-the-top support of this revolting group of people does have de facto advocacy of everything that they stand for, as well as complete awareness of everything that they had done.

Your later actions and words will cement this even further.

He was however, a very intelligent man and knew that he would have to appear to leave his repulsive racist beliefs in the past, when in actuality they would continue to be in the forefront of his brain, for his entire life.

As he ran for Congress in 1952, he started his decades long apology tour for his KKK days, while at the same time trying to whitewash much of his history.

This would prove to serve him well as he continued this disingenuous apology tour for decades to come with the same results. He would lie, people would choose to believe the lies, or not care about his past, and continue to vote him into office.

While there are a small percentage of people who can truly do a 180, and turn their life around, Byrd would repeatedly show that he was not one of those people, despite his well choreographed optics and political chess moves that he would play.

In 1957, Robert Byrd now entrenched in DC politics knew that sometimes apologies aren't good enough optics to fool people so he knew that he would have to do something extremely newsworthy, with the appearance of someone who had changed their stripes.

With this mindset, he voted for earlier versions of Civil Rights laws such as the 1957 Civil Rights Act as he knew that these earlier versions were watered down bills that did very little to help Black Americans, but were good for the optics to make it appear that something was being done.

Chess moves like this enabled him to take the next step up the political ladder as he ran for the Senate, and was elected, in 1958.

He continued his masquerade of someone who had changed, and in 1959, he hired one of the first black staffers as a congressional aide. He also did push for racial integration of the DC police department.

One question though, if he was so for blacks in the police department why didn't he have this done nationally as a civil right? That part will be answered later.

He would later use this methodology over and over again as although it looked good, it had very little actual significance to the day to day life of the average black person.

Later, there will be more instances of when he used slight of hand-misdirection, to appear that he was helping people with a different skin color from his, when in actuality that was all smoke and mirrors as nearly every chance he got to hurt blacks in this country, he made most of the opportunity.

THOMASYOUNG

CHAPTER SEVEN

This leads us to the groundbreaking, Civil Rights Act of 1964.

By 1964, racial tensions were growing in some areas of the country whereas other parts were more than ready to finally move forward, which led to the 1964 Civil Rights Act. There had been other smaller versions that had made incremental changes in the rights of all Americans, especially those in the black community, but noting overly significant.

Although more descript details from the bill will be discussed and shown later, including complete excerpts of the bill, a brief synopsis of the bill would include such major issues as the stoppage of the very racist Jim Crow laws that had been around since shortly after the being of the Civil War.

A brief summary and lead up to the bill is well-defined on History.com. From the website, it states,

'The Civil Rights Act of 1964, which ended segregation in public places and banned employment discrimination on the basis of race, color, religion, sex or national origin, is considered one of the crowning legislative achievements of the civil rights movement. First proposed by President John F. Kennedy, it survived strong opposition from southern members of Congress and was then signed into law by Kennedy's successor, Lyndon B. Johnson. In subsequent years, Congress expanded the act and passed additional civil rights legislation such as the Voting Rights Act of 1965.

Lead-up to the Civil Rights Act

Following the Civil War, a trio of constitutional amendments abolished slavery (the 13 Amendment), made the formerly enslaved people citizens (14 Amendment) and gave all men the right to vote regardless of race (15 Amendment).

Fifteenth Amendment

Nonetheless, many states—particularly in the South—used poll taxes, literacy tests and other measures to keep their African American citizens essentially disenfranchised. They also enforced strict segregation through "Jim Crow" laws and condoned violence from white supremacist groups like the Ku Klux Klan.

For decades after Reconstruction, the U.S. Congress did not pass a single civil rights act. Finally, in 1957, it established a civil rights section of the Justice Department, along with a Commission on Civil Rights to investigate discriminatory conditions.

Three years later, Congress provided for court-appointed referees to help Black people register to vote. Both of these bills were strongly watered down to overcome southern resistance.

When John F. Kennedy entered the White House in 1961, he initially delayed supporting new anti-discrimination measures. But with protests springing up throughout the South—including one in Birmingham, Alabama, where police brutally suppressed nonviolent demonstrators with dogs, clubs and high-pressure fire hoses—Kennedy decided to act.

In June 1963 he proposed by far the most comprehensive civil rights legislation to date, saying the United States "will not be fully free until all of its citizens are free."

Civil Rights Act Moves Through Congress

Kennedy was assassinated that November in Dallas,

after which new President Lyndon B. Johnson immediately took up the cause.

"Let this session of Congress be known as the session which did more for civil rights than the last hundred sessions combined," Johnson said in his first State of the Union address. During debate on the floor of the U.S. House of Representatives, southerners argued, among other things, that the bill unconstitutionally usurped individual liberties and states' rights.'

After passing through the House of Representatives with a bipartisan victory of 290-130 it moved to the Senate.

The History. com website would go on to speak of the Southern Democrat filibuster which attempted to thwart this bill that was much needed to become law.

It even specifically mentioned Robert Byrd by name (as well as his previous affiliation with the KKK) as one of the main leaders out to kill the bill, with a 14 plus hour filibuster of his own!

After some wrangling including an impassioned address on June 10, 1964 by Republican Senate Minority Leader Everett Dirksen of Illinois where he reminded his fellow Republicans that the

Republican Party stood for equality since it was founded just prior to the Civil War.

He also worked together with Democrat leader Hubert Humphrey to go against the racist Southern Democrats, like Byrd, and put an end to their attempted stoppage of the bill.

Fortunately good was victorious over bad as not only was the filibuster eventually broken but the new Civil Rights Act passed by a 73-27 vote in the Senate.

The bill became law on July 2, 1964, when signed by President Lyndon Johnson. Even then he knew that due to the Republican efforts to pass the bill it would be harsh on his fellow Democrats for years to come as was heard to have said, "It is an important gain, but I think we just delivered the South to the Republican Party for a long time to come".

Finally an official end to racial discrimination, Jim Crow laws and more, and not some watered down version such as the 1957 Civil Rights Law.

Why would anyone be against this, unless they were truly racist?

Over a decade after leaving the KKK, Byrd's true colors once again became more evident than ever.

Despite apologies and the occasional window dressing to give the appearance that he may have changed, when push comes to shove, with a chance to really help the black community his deep rooted hatred of that certain segment of the population rises to the top and it bursts out like water through a broken dam.

One still has to wonder why so many of the Democrats were against the bill?

Here is just one part of the bill from the official transcript of the bill itself.

This is from section 701 of the Civil Rights Act,

'TITLE VII--EQUAL EMPLOYMENT OPPORTUNITY

DEFINITIONS

SEC. 701. For the purposes of this title--

(a) The term "person" includes one or more individuals, labor unions, partnerships, associations, corporations, legal representatives, mutual companies, joint-stock companies, trusts, unincorporated organizations, trustees, trustees in bankruptcy, or receivers.

(b) The term "employer" means a person engaged in an industry affecting commerce who has twenty-five or more employees for each working day in each of twenty or more calendar weeks in the current or preceding calendar year, and any agent of such a person, but such term does not include (1) the United States, a corporation wholly owned by the Government of the United States, an Indian tribe, or a State or political subdivision thereof, (2) a bona fide private membership club (other than a labor organization) which is exempt from taxation under section 501(c) of the Internal Revenue Code of 1954: Provided, That during the first year after the effective date prescribed in subsection (a) of section 716, persons having fewer than one hundred employees (and their agents) shall not be considered employers, and, during the second year after such date, persons having fewer than seventy-five employees (and their agents) shall not be considered employers, and, during the third year after such date, persons having fewer than fifty employees (and their agents) shall not be considered employers: Provided further, That it shall be the policy of the United States to insure equal employment opportunities for Federal employees without discrimination because of race, color, religion, sex or national origin and the President shall utilize his existing authority to effectuate this policy.

(c) The term "employment agency" means any person regularly undertaking with or without compensation to procure employees for an employer or to procure for employees opportunities to work for an employer and includes an agent of such a person; but shall not include an agency of the United States, or an agency of a State or political subdivision of a State, except that such term shall

include the United States Employment Service and the system of State and local employment services receiving Federal assistance.

(d) The term "labor organization" means a labor organization engaged in an industry affecting commerce, and any agent of such an organization, and includes any organization of any kind, any

agency, or employee representation committee, group, association, or plan so engaged in which employees participate and which exists for the purpose, in whole or in part, of dealing with employers concerning grievances, labor disputes, wages, rates of pay, hours, or other terms or conditions of employment, and any conference, general committee, joint or system board, or joint council so engaged which is subordinate to a national or international labor organization.

(e) A labor organization shall be deemed to be engaged in an industry affecting commerce if (1) it maintains or operates a hiring hall or hiring office which procures employees for an employer or procures for employees opportunities to work for an employer, or (2) the number of its members (or, where it is a labor organization composed of other labor organizations or their representatives, if the aggregate number of the members of such other labor organization) is (A) one hundred or more during the first year after the effective date prescribed in subsection (a) of section 716, (B) seventy-five or more during the second year after such date or fifty or more during the third year, or (C) twenty-five or more thereafter, and such labor organization--

(1) is the certified representative of employees under the provisions of the National Labor Relations Act, as amended, or the Railway Labor Act, as amended;

(2) although not certified, is a national or international labor organization or a local labor organization recognized or acting as the representative of employees of an employer or employers engaged in an industry affecting commerce; or

3) has chartered a local labor organization or subsidiary body which is representing or actively seeking to represent employees of employers within the meaning of paragraph (1) or (2); or

(4) has been chartered by a labor organization representing or actively seeking to represent employees within the meaning of paragraph (1) or (2) as the local or subordinate body through which such employees may enjoy membership or become affiliated with such labor organization; or

(5) is a conference, general committee, joint or system board, or joint council subordinate to a

national or international labor organization, which includes a labor organization engaged in an industry affecting commerce within the meaning of any of the preceding paragraphs of this subsection.

(f) The term "employee" means an individual employed by an employer.

(g) The term "commerce" means trade, traffic, commerce, transportation, transmission, or communication among the several States; or between a State and any place outside thereof; or within the District of Columbia, or a possession of the United States; or between points in the same State but through a point outside thereof.

(h) The term "industry affecting commerce" means any activity, business, or industry in commerce or in which a labor dispute would hinder or obstruct commerce or the free flow of commerce and includes any activity or industry "affecting commerce" within the meaning of the Labor-Management Reporting and Disclosure Act of 1959.

(i) The term "State" includes a State of the United States, the District of Columbia, Puerto Rico, the Virgin Islands, American Samoa, Guam, Wake Island, The Canal Zone, and Outer Continental Shelf lands defined in the Outer Continental Shelf Lands

Act.'

That was just a taste of the new law. It shows that anyone opposed to this must have an immense amount of racial hatred flowing through their veins.

Unfortunately for this country, even after the passage of the Civil Rights Act, the repulsive, racist Democrats still tried to use their power and influence to hinder the advancement of Black Americans.

By 1965, Byrd's deep hatred of blacks in the country was more evident than ever.

With the memory of his vehement opposition to the 1964 Civil Rights Act, that was shot down, still fresh in his mind, his racist rhetoric once again showed itself. This time it was on one of the most racist speeches in a generation on the Senate floor.

Near the end of 1965, Byrd sounded off on the black trouble in the cities as he said, "The ghettos are blamed; yet, people of all races have lived in ghettos in the past; but they have not rioted. Poverty is blamed for the riots; yet poverty-stricken whites outnumber poverty stricken Negroes in America, but they are not rioting. We can take the people out of the slums, but we cannot take the slums out of the people."

If that wasn't enough, Byrd's words about Civil Rights Icon Dr Martin Luther King Jr continued his hateful trend as he said that Dr King was nothing more than a "rabble-rouser".

To top that off, just days prior to the April 4, 1968 assassination, of Dr Martin Luther King Jr, Byrd gave a fiery anti-MLK speech that one can only wonder what was the ripple effect, or possibly the direct effect of his hateful statement.

On March 29, 1968, Byrd lambasted a protest in the same Memphis, Tennessee town where Dr King violently had his life taken from him, as he said, "It was a shameful and totally uncalled for outburst of lawlessness undoubtedly encouraged to some considerable degree, at least, by his words and actions, and his presence. There is no reason for us to believe that the same destructive rioting and violence cannot, or that it will not, happen here if King attempts his so-called Poor People's March, for what he plans in Washington appears to be something on a far greater scale than what he had indicated he planned to do in Memphis".

Less than a week later, MLK had his last breath permanently taken from him in that very same town.

This can hardly be just a coincidence. The man that a very vociferous, Senator Robert Byrd blasted on the Senate floor, called a "rabble-rouser ", then just before he was murdered, was the recipient of more hateful, antagonist rhetoric from the same, high-profile, Senator Byrd.

After the murder of Dr King, he was hardly

apologetic for his earlier remarks. In fact, he doubled-down on them as of he was proud of what he said as he asked what did people expect from someone who stirs up trouble like King did.

Where was the investigation into Byrd after King was assassinated directly after Byrd's almost urging of that outcome? He liked investigating others. How come there was no in-depth discussion about any possible involvement, whether directly, or indirectly?

Where were the Woodward and Bernstein wannabes then, and in the decades that followed?

They all seem more comfortable creating controversy and their fictional version of so-called facts than to actually report truths.

The facts are that Byrd said did horrific things at a time when racial problems were about to turn better in this country.

He tried to do everything in his power, for years and years to stop that from happening, which includes his verbal tirades against Dr King up to days before his tragic death.

It would be nice if reporters in today's world would've brought that up to Joe Biden in 2020, when he was on his way to becoming my the next President of the United States.

After all, Byrd was his mentor and best friend.

But even back in the 1960's many of the

hateful Democrats were able to have their racist transgressions covered up.

Maybe, years later, if someone had brought up those facts about Byrd and Dr King, maybe it would've forced public outcry and an investigation. Yes, it would've been decades too late, but it would've been nice to know the truth, the real truth.

Also, after Martin Luther King Jr. was assassinated Byrd's answer to the riots that followed by actually suggesting that the United States military should kill the black protesters who got rowdy.

Then again, this is the same Democratic Senator Robert Byrd who at one time suggested that Dr King not be allowed in Washington DC.

His exact words about the rioters were, "If it requires the Army, Navy, Air Force, Marines, we should put the troublemakers in their places." He added that looters should be shot on the spot, "swiftly and mercilessly."

Now, I'm all for stopping violence in protests. Why not have the police arrest the violent protesters, looters, etc., while letting the non-violent ones who are simply speaking their minds have their say?

If that technique had been used decades later on 2020, there would've been fewer problems, fewer deaths but an example would've been made by having those who broke the law go to jail, and unlike Robert Byrd, not suggest murdering them since they were black.

But instead, total chaos was allowed to spread for months in 2020.

Someone like Byrd could've set a powerful example back in the 1960's with a simple solution (and yes have the National Guard ready if needed) of arresting the ones who broke the law and not make things worse by suggesting that they be executed on the streets.

In addition to that, in the same year, 1968, during Democratic Party presidential primaries, Byrd supported President Lyndon Johnson in his bid for re-election.

His challenger was Robert F. Kennedy, whose brother John F Kennedy was slain several years earlier.

Of Bobby Kennedy, Byrd said, "Bobby-come-lately has made a mistake. I won't even listen to him. There are many who liked his brother—as Bobby will find out—but who don't like him."

On June 5, 1968, he too was murdered. Could it be just a coincidence that two people that Byrd not only very much disliked and chose words that almost requested that they be eliminated, were both assassinated shortly after his fiery rhetoric?

We don't know.

Lyndon Johnson, another racist Democrat, no longer had his toughest competition.

Should there have been an investigation?

Yes, definitely, but unfortunately that never happened and Byrd was able to continue his abysmal ways which included his desire to quench his racist thirst as there was a Supreme Court nomination for the first black man to reach the highest court in the land.

Thurgood Marshall was sworn into office in 1968 despite the objection from Byrd, and others.

THE REPUBLICAN PARTY: FORMED IN 1854 TO END SLAVER...

CHAPTER EIGHT

There were many other of the racist Democrats who were making it tough on Black Americans. More on them to come. Back to Robert Byrd. Remember back when he was making those symbolic moves back in the 1950's to give the appearance that he had changed just so that he could get elected.

That was obvious more subterfuge as once he was entrenched into the senate he was able to return to his hateful roots more out in the open.

At least for awhile he could do that until years later he would once again have to give the facade that he had changed.

But until then, and we after then, he knew that he just had to give empty apologies at the right tines and to the right people and he would have no problem getting re-elected over and over again.

By the time the 1970's arrived, there were others who were those in Congress, more specifically in the Senate who looked up to him and admired him.

Robert Byrd had a great deal of influence on these members of Congress. One of, if not the most notable, was then-Senator (who in 2020 was elected President) Joe Biden.

Biden often called Byrd his mentor and good friend.

The way that Biden took a cue from Byrd in a myriad of ways amplified this even further.

One such case, was when Biden allowed his inner racism to shine through, when with the help of other segregationists, he helped write multiple segregation bills in the 1970's.

One of those bills, H.R. 1950, the Anti-busing Act, was passed, and became law in 1975. Like Byrd, Biden was learning the political game of talking out of both sides of the mouth.

The law was aimed at keeping black kids out of white schools because as Biden put it, he didn't want the schools to become a "racial jungle".

Biden claimed that he wasn't against desegregation but rather against the busing of the kids to the schools.

But Biden knew that Busing was at the core if desegregation. Having desegregation without busing was like having apple pie without the apples.

Biden isn't the smartest apple on the tree but he was smart enough to learn how to spread racism from someone who actually was cunning and a con artist, Senator Robert Byrd.

Like much of what Byrd touched himself, or influenced, this had years of negative consequences for many blacks across the country who were denied a better education purely because of their shin color.

Byrd's radical racial influence of Biden wasn't only strong on the 1970's, but it also followed him throughout much of his career. More on that later.

The funny thing is that despite all of the years of harm that Byrd and his protege, Joe Biden, did to thousands, possibly millions of Black Americans in their lifetimes, the liberals of today, as well as most of the mainstream media, who are quick to point the racist finger at the other side, many times erroneously, way too often give Byrd and his compadre a pass for the decades of harm that they have caused.

In 1999, a Gallop poll was done about school integration. 80% of the younger generation thought that integration programs worked.

That's an astounding number.

Unfortunately Biden, even as of 2024, in his heart doesn't feel this way as he would rather Black kids be forced to go to horrible schools, some with proficiency ratings as low as ZERO PERCENT!

Yes, in some cases, 0%!

Senator Tim Scott, back in the Trump Presidency years, introduced school choice where the federal dollars follow the student and don't go directly to schools.

This allows students from any socio-economic background, regardless of race, sex, etc., to go to the school of their choice, whether public or charter.

Many states have had tremendous success with the program. Instead of students, especially those in bad schools, many of whom are black, having to go to bad schools, these students now are able to go to good schools, get a good education and not be stuck in an endless cycle of failure which those like Byrd's protege, Joe Biden have preferred over the years.

Many people think that the now-President Joe Biden, who wanders, or rambles on aimlessly is just an old man who has begun to lose cognizance. Many have depicted him as a kindly old man who should just be sitting in his rocking chair on a front porch drinking a glass of lemonade.

Although his obvious loss of cognizant abilities is apparent to anyone with even a touch of impartiality, the kindly old man reference is not an accurate description for those that have closely followed him for decades.

The real Joe Biden is another Democrat with a long history of racism, lies, incompetence, and unfortunately more.

It's odd how Biden has claimed that he "doesn't have a racist bone in his body," when his actions, and words say otherwise.

From the 1970's through his Presidency, he has said/done so many racist things that's its almost impossible to account for them all.

Voted into office in 1972, then-Senator Biden took little time to show what he was all about.

In the 1970's he worked with staunch racist segregationists to author two segregation bills,

one of which became law.

Biden authored an amendment to an appropriations bill in 1975 that stopped the government from withholding federal funds from schools that stayed segregated. This amendment included schools that didn't even use busing. In other words, any school, regardless of whether they were part of the busing issue or not, would be able to intentionally separate students by race, and still get government funding.

The amendment passed, with the help of other segregationists, and eventually became law. Biden tweaked an earlier version of a bill that was written by segregationists, so that it would pass.

He attempted to author yet another segregation bill two years later. That bill however, failed to pass through Congress.

He said that he was for civil rights, and against segregation as a whole, but was against the busing of students into schools. For instance, he was against black kids being bused into mostly white schools.

He tried to play both sides of the fence of the segregation issue, but his logic, much like much of his career, made no sense.

He even had the infamous "racial jungle" quote, which he said at a Senate Judiciary Committee in 1977, while speaking on the subject of school segregation and busing:

"Unless we do something about this, my children are going to grow up in a jungle, the jungle being a racial jungle with tensions having built so high that it is going to explode at some point. We have got to make some move on this".

Later statistics have shown that he was wrong (a common theme) to take the stance on busing that he did. His racism (again, unfortunately a common theme) led him astray.

Statistics, and studies such as a 2011 study by Berkeley professor, Rucker Johnson have shown that his overt racism was sorely misplaced, as research showed that the black kids that were bused into predominantly white schools did better academically, health wise, and even reduced the chances of them going to jail, while those who were unable to, or chose not to, participate in the program, did worse.

His continued explanation of his stance is so idiotic that a 3-year old could see through it.

He said that he was for desegregation, but against busing, which is like one saying that they would like apple pie, if they took out the apples.

Busing, like apples in the analogy, was the centerpiece of desegregation in schools. Without it, there was no desegregation, and backs and whites would continue to be separated from each other in many cases.

Although he isn't a brilliant man, Biden is smart enough to know this, as he learned from his racist allies, how to play both sides of an issue.

In 1977, President Jimmy Carter nominated two black men, Drew Days III And Wade McCree, Both Black Men, to DOJ Positions. They were both for busing as part of desegregation. They breezed through the Senate Judiciary Committee to eventually becoming confirmed by the Senate, despite Biden's objections. Biden voted against their

nomination while on the Senate floor claiming, 'I voted against them because we seem to disagree over an issue of great concern to me and the citizens of Delaware. The issue is forced busing. I oppose it. The citizens of Delaware oppose it. And, if my instincts are correct, the people in this nation oppose it."

Even though the truth was staring him right in the face, he refused to yield to his segregation ways.

Was it his pettiness, or pure racism that sought to deny this monumental achievement for the black community, and civil rights in general?

Drew Days III became the first black head of the department's civil rights division in this country's history, and Wade McCree became the second black solicitor general, after they were both confirmed.

That is a huge deal. But this person named Joe Biden, who continually claimed he was for blacks and civil rights, used excuse after excuse to continually attempt to keep them down.

From early on as a Senator, Biden learned a great deal from his racist buddies.

One of Biden's closest allies, and friends, was none other than former KKK leader, Senator Robert Byrd.

Biden would not only call Byrd his friend, but also his mentor. At Byrd's funeral, he would give a lengthy eulogy of the man who was an extremely hateful racist for decades, and actually said that he was a "great man".

Imagine for a second if this had been a Republican (especially Trump) who had a friend, mentor, ally, and associate, such as Byrd, instead of Biden.

Then there are some outrageous quotes from Biden. When reading these, imagine if someone like former President Trump, Florida Governor Ron DeSantis, or other prominent Republicans had said any of these, much less, all of them.

There was the previously mentioned "racist jungle quote", as well as many, many others.

Everyone has heard Biden's "you ain't black" quote. Here are more of his racist quotes:

August of 2020,

"Unlike the African-American community, with notable exceptions, the Latino community is an incredibly diverse community with incredibly diverse attitudes about different things."

On why he was able to stay at home during the Covid pandemic, he said,

"They're saying, 'Jeez, the reason I was able to stay sequestered in my home is because some Black woman was able to stack the grocery shelf'".

In August of 2019, at a campaign event in Iowa, "poor kids are just as bright and talented as white kids."

With Joe, being poor automatically equates to being black.

On January 31, 2007, during his presidential campaign he said of then Senator Barack Obama "I mean, you got the first mainstream African-American who is articulate and bright and clean and a nice-looking guy. I mean, that's a storybook, man."

Apparently to Biden being black and also "articulate, bright and clean," are usually mutually exclusive.

In real life, this isn't the case, of course. However in Biden's feeble, narrow minded racist brain, being black, well spoken and intelligent is a rarity. Talk about the textbook definition of racism.

On June 17th, 2006, when he was a Delaware senator he made this very degrading comment, "In Delaware, the largest growth in population is Indian Americans, moving from India. You cannot go to a 7-11 or a Dunkin Donuts unless you have a slight Indian accent. I'm not joking."

There was the earlier mentioned racial jungle quote, with regards to busing and segregation.

At a birthday party, in 1985, for Senator John C. Stennis, who had a long history in opposing civil rights, "He is the rockbed of integrity of the United States Congress."

In June of 2019, Biden denied an accusation from Kamala Harris that he had previously praised segregationists.

His response was yet another flat out lie, when he said, "It's a mischaracterization of my position across the board. I did not praise racists. That is not true,"

Over the years, though, Biden has repeatedly praised segregationists like John Stennis, Senator James Eastland, Senator Herman Talmadge and others.

These Democrats were the epitome of racists. They all attempted to use their power against Black Americans.

Biden was all to happy to cozy up to them.

At the previously mentioned birthday party for Stennis, in 1985, Biden heaped on second helpings of praise for the segregationist, birthday boy Stennis, when he said, "He's an opponent without hate, a friend without treachery, a statesman without pretense, a victim without any murmuring, a public official without vice, a private citizen without wrong, a neighbor, as you all know, without hypocrisy, a man without guilt. A senator whom future senators can study with profit for as long as there is an America."

Stennis, who was against the Civil Rights Acts of 1958, as well as 1964, was also a staunch segregationist. He continued his racist ways into the 1980's as in 1983 he was the only southern Democrat to vote against making Martin Luther King Jr. Day a national holiday. In fact only three other Democrats total, voted against the future national holiday.

Biden would call Stennis both "a very honorable man", and "a friend".

Joe, I would call this, as well as all of the other positive comments that you've made towards racists and segregationists, as "praise"!

Then there is the man (I use that term loosely), Senate James Eastland who Biden worked with to derail busing, and write a segregation bill.

Here are actual despicable comments made by Eastland at an event in the 1950's. I cut out part of a disgusting word that I despise. Although I edited it, Eastland did not.

"In every stage of the bus boycott we have been oppressed and degraded because of black, slimy, juicy, unbearably stinking ni**ers".

He added,

"When in the course of human events it becomes necessary to abolish the Negro race, proper methods should be used"

Eastland went as far as to say,

"All whites are created equal with certain rights, among these are life, liberty and the pursuit of dead ni**ers".

Many have thanked historian Robert Caro for bringing this piece of information to light. Despite the repulsive rhetoric from Eastland, it's good to have people like Caro to share the truth, even when ugly.

Their racist efforts didn't work, as the public was still outraged over the hideous crime by the white supremacists, by their actions of continually siding against basic civil rights says a lot about them.

In spring of 1956, Stennis and Eastland signed onto

the Southern Manifesto, which soundly denounced the Supreme Court's desegregation orders following the Court's 1954 decision in Brown v. Board of Education of Topeka, Kansas.

The U.S. Supreme Court declared that state laws establishing separate public schools for students of different races to be unconstitutional.

They called it a "clear abuse of judicial powers."

Stennis helped write the Manifesto along with fellow segregationist Sen. Strom Thurmond.

Eastland loudly proclaimed that integration would result in lower education standards.

That's moronic of course but what do you expect from such extreme racists.

These same Senators would go on to help Biden in his own efforts to keep schools segregated.

In 1977, Biden write to Senator Eastland twice thanking him to help stop the busing and desegregation in schools.

Later, Biden invited Eastland who was known for his fiery speeches to speak on the Senate floor in support of his legislation.

On Aug. 22, 1978, Biden wrote, "I want to personally ask your continued support and alert you to our intentions. He added that, "Your participation in floor debate would be welcomed."

He not only worked with extreme racists, he openly

asked for their help, and on many occasions praised them.

I fathom to guess the ballistic outrage that would be happening if one-tenth of this had come from a prominent Republican like Donald Trump, Ron DeSantis, or Ted Cruz, among others.

After working with Biden to try and stop desegregation, Eastland would later help Biden get his position on the Foreign Relations Committee.

Biden also bragged about an award that he had gotten from extremely racist, Alabama governor, George Wallace.

Wallace praised him as one of the outstanding young politicians of America.

Wallace, the former Alabama Governor has been widely associated with the hardcore racism of decades ago.

At the conclusion of his initial inauguration, the Democratic Senator, he had the infamous line,

"Segregation now, segregation tomorrow, segregation forever."

In 1963, at another event, Wallace led what some would later call, "stand-in the schoolhouse door" to prevent two black students from enrolling at the University of Alabama.

It was so bad that President John F. Kennedy had to call for troops from the Alabama National Guard to help federal officials, to get Wallace to move.

Wallace would continue his racist actions and comments for many years to come.

Like Democratic Senator Robert Byrd, Wallace would later apologize for some of his racist comments and actions. Political expediency is very popular with these racist, hateful politicians.

While some accepted it, most of Wallace's detractors smelled something fishy with his sudden turn.

Like with Byrd, and while some people do change, I find it extremely difficult to believe that someone with that much excruciating racist hatred can suddenly overnight realize "Oh, racism is bad, sorry"!

Biden's true colors come shining through when he doesn't have time to think of a way to be politically correct.

Other times he just plain lies as if it's second nature.

This is especially bad when it comes to racism, and racial subjects in general.

During the 1988 Presidential campaign he told so many lies that its hard to keep up with them all.

Some were about his qualifications, including schooling, some were about race, such as when he fictitiously bragged about marching for civil rights.

He was up in New Hampshire in February of 1987, when he falsely boasted, "When I marched in the civil rights movement, I did not march with a 12-point program."

He compounded this lie by adding, "I marched with tens of thousands of others to change attitudes. And we changed attitudes."

He had repeated this "marching" lie, as he is prone to do, multiple times during that campaign.

He later mutated that lie in a story claiming that he marched for Civil Rights in Selma, Alabama.

Not only had he never traveled to Selma, Alabama, he had not visited anywhere near there, nor any Southern state in that timeframe.

Eventually Biden admitted that these statements weren't true. In August of 1987 he said, "During the 60's, I was in fact very concerned about the civil rights movement. I was not an activist, I worked at an all-black swimming pool in the east side of Wilmington, Delaware. I was involved. I was involved in what they were thinking, what they were feeling. I was involved, but I was not out marching. I was not down in Selma. I was not anywhere else. I was a suburbanite kid who got a dose of exposure to what was happening to black Americans in my own city".

Some of his statements may be racist, while others show how he flat out lies while attempting to show that he's not racist.

In June of 2019, while attempting to show that he wasn't racist, he said that he was civil towards those that he claimed were on the opposite side of the aisle. History has shown however, that not only as he been civil with them, but he has also worked closely with them to help achieve their racist schemes, as well as doting on their friendships and accolades.

In February of 2020, Biden told yet another astronomically huge lie in South Carolina, about back when he was a Senator, and attempting to see Nelson Mandela, in South Africa.

Biden said, "This day, 30 years ago, Nelson Mandela walked out of prison and entered into discussions about apartheid".

He went onto say, "I had the great honor of meeting him. I had the great honor of being arrested with our U.N. ambassador on the streets of Soweto".

Later, while in Las Vegas, he extended the complete fabrication, as he said this about Mandela,

"He threw his arms around me and said, 'I want to say thank you'".

That still wasn't enough for Joe as he continued to extend the lie as he said,

"I said, 'What are you thanking me for, Mr. President?' He said: 'You tried to see me. You got arrested trying to see me.' "

It's not enough that he initially lied. But to make matters worse, he not only repeated the falsehood, but he added on to the completely fictionalized story.

The U.S. ambassador, Andrew Young, who was with

Biden during the South Africa trip had said that he wasn't arrested and didn't think that Biden was either.

Biden thought that he could spread this race related tale as he pandered towards getting black votes, as unfortunately Mandela had passed away in 2013. It's easy to lie about someone who isn't here to prove you wrong, right? That's pretty slimy, but then again, that's Joe.

His campaign eventually admitted that he had lied, although they had to put a spin on the truth. There seems to be so much spin with Biden that if he ever shot pool, he would be a shark with all of the English on the ball.

Biden's deputy campaign manager, Kate Bedingfield later would say that Biden was talking about the time when he was at Johannesburg airport, when he had been separated from other parts of his party, as he wasn't allowed to go through the same door as the rest of his party.

Back in 2013, Joe had said, "When I exited the plane I was directed to one side of the tarmac, while the African American congressmen travelling with me were sent to the other side. I refused to break off, and the officials finally relented."

So Joe, how does you wanting to go through the same door as the black congressmen that were with you, come even close to being arrested? It doesn't of course. And by the way Joe, most average people would also stand up and go through the same door as the black people they were with. The difference is that they wouldn't expect some type of accolades for simply doing the right thing.

By your asking for applause Joe, makes one question if you were doing this to be an average human being, or as simply another chance at race pandering?

By saying one thing in 2013, and then another, then including your extraordinary lie 7 years later, after the passing of Mandela, gives us a pretty good idea of your intentions.

In 1993, during the confirmation hearing of Supreme Court Justice Ruth Bader Ginsburg, Senator Biden responded to other comments about Senator Howell Heflin's Senate speech, where Joe said, "I too, heard that speech and, for the public listening to this, the Senator made a very moving and eloquent speech, as a son of the Confederacy, acknowledging that it was time to change and yield to a position that Senator Carol Moseley-Braun raised on the Senate floor, not granting a Federal charter to an organization made up of many fine people who continue to display the Confederate flag as a symbol".

He also voted to restore the citizenship of Confederate leaders, Robert E. Lee, in 1975, and later Jefferson Davis, in 1977.

As much as there is a whirlwind around supporting anything to do with the Confederacy, how has he not been lambasted over this?

Biden's biggest piece of legislation that he was a part of that passed, was now infamous 1994 crime bill. This bill, which became the Violent Crime Control and Law Enforcement Act of 1994, was co-authored by Senators Biden, and Orrin Hatch.

This law overwhelmingly adversely affected black Americans, as many were jailed in lengthy prison sentences on often petty crimes.

While speaking to Congress about the bill on November 18, 1993, Biden said,

"We have predators on our streets that society has in fact, in part because of its neglect, created...they are beyond the pale many of those people, beyond the pale. And it's a sad commentary on society. We have no choice but to take them out of society....a cadre of young people, tens of thousands of them, born out of wedlock, without parents, without supervision, without any structure, without any conscience developing because they literally ... because they literally have not been socialized, they literally have not had an opportunity....we should focus on them now....if we don't, they will, or a portion of them, will become the predators fifteen years from now."

While Biden didn't directly say "black people", it's obvious who is talking about when he refers to "predators", and what they will do, as the overwhelming, disproportionate number of people who were affected by this bill, that became law, were black Americans.

One of the clear racist elements of the bill was the difference in the sentences in crack cocaine versus powder. Powder cocaine was used more by white people than black, but those convicted of crack cocaine often received harsher sentences.

The bill also included "three strikes and you're out", which imprisoned those who committed minor drug offenses, as well as ordering mandatory minimum sentences.

More from Biden's impassioned speech included,

"We must make the streets safer. I don't care why someone is a malefactor in society. I don't care why someone is anti-social. I don't care why they become a sociopath. We have an obligation to cordon them off from the rest of society, try to help them, try to change their behavior".

Although it was sold as an anti-crime bill to Congress and the public, the wording of the bill, as well as Biden's own inflammatory comments, show that Biden directly intended this bill to hurt one group of people.

More of his language from that speech, on the bill, drove home his racist intent even more. He didn't have to directly say the words, as his intentions were clear, with statements such as,

"It doesn't matter whether or not the person that is accosting your son or daughter or my son or daughter, my wife, your husband, my mother, your parents, it doesn't matter whether or not they were deprived as a youth. It doesn't matter whether or not they had no background that enabled them to become socialized into the fabric of society. It doesn't matter whether or not they're the victims of society. The end result is they're about to knock my mother on the head with a lead pipe, shoot my sister, beat up my wife, take on my sons."

One of the things that Biden was best at, was unfortunately the hurting of black Americans under the guise of doing the right thing.

He did that with his segregation stance, continued through doing it in the 80's, the 90's, and beyond.

Biden has repeated the "very fine people" lie over and over again about President Trump and the Charlottesville riot in August of 2017.

Biden has repeatedly said since announcing his candidacy for President in 2019 that he knew that he had to run for President after Charlottesville and hearing President Trump's response to the riot.

He has continually claimed that Trump called the white Nationalists that were there 'very fine people".

That's not at all what Trump said, but that hasn't deterred him from continuing the lie.

Biden later repeated this racist lie when he said,

"He said there were, quote, 'very fine people on both sides'. That was a wake-up call for us as a country and for me a call to action."

Even many usually liberal fact checkers and media outlets have told the truth and have repeated that wasn't what Trump had actually said.

What's worse, being a racist, or falsely accusing someone else of being one?

CHAPTER NINE

From Biden's extraordinarily racist buddies that he worked closely with, and who enormously helped his career, to his racist actions, to his racist statements, this is not a good man.

Of course, during the mid to late 1900's, there were some good Democrats, like MLK, Thurgood Marshall, and others who did try and help Black Americans but often it was their fellow Democrats, like Robert Byrd, and many others who tried to silence their voices and actions.

There were also a few on the Republican side like Senator Strom Thurmond who went from Democrat to Republican who were Republican. No side is perfect.

But all too often it was those in the Democratic Party who not only tried to make things worse for

Black Americans but were allowed to continue these efforts with the backing of their party.

In October of 1991, Republican President George H. W. Bush's Supreme Court nominee, Clarence Thomas was sworn in, replacing the retiring Marshall.

One would think that a black Justice replacing the previous first black Justice was a good thing.

But not to the Democrats.

This was especially true to Senator Robert Byrd, who once again showed his anti-black he was as he became the only Senator to ever vote against the first two black Justices, when he voted against Thomas making it to the Supreme Court.

By the 1990's even some organizations that used to champion Civil Rights became nothing more than political pawns.

One such case was the NAACP. They went from trying to help Black Americans to turning their backs on them when politics dictated.

They actually opposed a highly qualified black man replacing a black man on the Supreme Court.

They weren't the only Civil Rights activists who became frauds who were only in it for themselves.

Others like Jesse Jackson and Al Sharpton would spend the next several decades sowing racial division instead of real unity. If there was real unity then they would be out of business and they knew it.

Other Democrats took notice and that would be their marketing tool for years, and decades to come.

The would masquerade as helping the black community, when all they would do is make things worse, and then blame the other side.

That proved to be a highly effective way to keep power and make money as every time that Republicans tried to help Black Americans they were called ugly names and were shunned.

In 2015, however a man by the name of Donald J. Trump through his hat in the ring as he announced his candidacy for the President of the United States.

He was mocked and called vicious lies, but he wanted to help all Americans especially those who he felt were being neglected which included Black Americans.

The opposition (Democrats and the mainstream media) didn't like that their grift may get terminated and tried every underhanded scheme to stop him.

Fortunately for Black Americans, and all Americans, he still was able to win the Presidential election of 2016.

There were a plethora of ways that this Republican was able to help Black Americans..

It was President Trump that tried to undo the damage of Biden's co-authored 1994 crime bill.

Trump actually to fix the problem, something that

Biden never did, even when he was Vice President under President Obama.

Trump spear-headed the prison reform bill to be known as the First Step Act.

This bipartisan bill greatly reduced unjust sentences that were had been given to non-violent offenders. A large percentage of these people were black Americans.

In July of 2019, the law allowed the release of over 3,000 Americans, a vast majority of whom were black Americans.

Other parts in the law included getting rid of the "three strikes" life sentencing provision in some cases, so that many non-violent offenders wouldn't spend the rest of their lives in jail.

Trump was even given the Bipartisan Justice Award for his work with the First Step Act.

A White House press release back in 2019 said,

"The 2019 Bipartisan Justice award winner is President Donald J. Trump for his Bipartisan leadership in the passage of the historic First Step Act."

It added that, "The award is being given by the 20/20 Bipartisan Justice Center, a non-profit organization founded by 20 Black Republicans and 20 Black Democrats in 2015, to elevate the issue of criminal justice reform above partisan politics".

So basically black leaders from both sides of the

aisle, gave Trump an award where he helped clean up Biden's mess from the errors embedded in the 1994 crime bill that he had co-authored.

Also under Trump (and before Covid) there was a record low unemployment rate among Black and Hispanic Americans.

Trump had promised to help minority students and he delivered on that promise.

On December 19, 2021, Trump signed the FUTURE Act, which made permanent $255 million in annual STEM funding for minority-serving colleges, which included around 85 million directly earmarked for HBCU's (Historically Black Colleges and Universities).

After Biden became President, he miraculously realized that there was a need for this type of funding. It's odd that in all of his years in the Senate, he didn't think that a huge amount like this was necessary.

After he took office however, and being reminded of Trump's enormous amount of permanent funding for minority students, Biden suddenly felt the political need to perform a similar action.

Trump worked with Senator Tim Scott on two separate initiatives to help the black community.

Biden of course didn't start any of these when he was a Senator.

The first thing was school choice. Trump and

Senator Scott worked together to build a program where kids at failing schools would have the opportunity to go to better schools, and not automatically stuck in the same system that wasn't working.

The second thing that Trump and Senator Scott worked on to help the black community were opportunity zones. I wonder why Biden never thought about that?

Opportunityzones.org described this endeavor that was as part of the 2017 Tax Cuts and Jobs Act, as "An Opportunity Zone is a powerful new tool intended to stimulate investment in distressed communities".

According to HUD (Department of Housing an Urban Development) from August 25, 2020, The Council of Economic Advisers (CEA) "estimates that Opportunity Zones have already generated approximately half a million jobs, attracted $75 billion in capital investments, and are on track to reduce the poverty rate in Opportunity Zones by 11 percent-lifting 1,000,000 people out of poverty".

Also from the HUD website, The CEA report said that

"From the second quarter of 2018 to the fourth quarter of 2019, private equity investments into Opportunity Zone businesses grew 29% relative to a comparable set of businesses not in Opportunity Zones.

Investments in Opportunity Zones will lift approximately one million Americans from poverty.

The poverty rate in Opportunity Zones will decrease by 11%.

An Opportunity Zone designation alone has increased private property values within the designated areas by 1.1%. For the nearly half of Opportunity Zone residents who own their own homes, the increase provides an estimated $11 billion in new wealth."

Wow! Again Joe, in all of your years of public service, why didn't you think of helping the black community like that?

In September, of 2020, President Trump rolled out his "Platinum Plan".

As part of his Platinum Plan, that was planned for his second term, Trump proposed to have the KKK prosecuted as domestic terrorists.

He has repeatedly condemned the KKK and white supremacy as a whole.

In fact, back in August of 2019 he had said, "In one voice, our nation must condemn racism, bigotry, and white supremacy. These sinister ideologies must be defeated. Hate has no place in America. Hatred warps the mind, ravages the heart, and devours the soul."

How come Biden didn't push for the KKK to be listed as domestic terrorists? Could it be that it would mean that some of his buddies would had been labeled as domestic terrorists?

Unfortunately, Biden was somehow able to defeat Trump and the lives of many Americans, especially those in the black community were greatly, adversely affected.

Democrat run cities are a great example of this. For decades they have been a haven for crime and rundown conditions.

As Covid taught us, Democrat leaders wanted to keep those in the cities locked down and under their control.

Even after Covid, they still want that control. They've been playing the control game for decades, but now many are seeing what is happening.

The earlier mentioned policies from Trump, such as Opportunity Zones and School Choice helped those in the inner cities and can help once again. There are more ways that he had helped of course such as lower taxes, higher wages, and record amount of funding to HBCUs and more.

Policies like these directly helped those in the black community.

It wasn't just decades of empty rhetoric aimed at securing votes from Black Americans.

Policies like these showed once again that the leaders in the Republican Party wanted to help those in the black community by not giving them a free handout, but by allowing them to help themselves.

Unlike many of the Democratic leaders, many on

the Republican side know that those in the black community don't need to be given things to them based solely on their skin color.

They know that that every American is fully capable of good things, whether they are black, white, Hispanic, etc.

They don't need programs like DEI (Diversity, Equity and Inclusion) which uses ones skin color, sexuality, etc., as the top metric for hiring, advancement, etc.

Republicans know that it's equality and not equity that matters and that every person should be given their opportunity based on merit and not because they check a box.

This ensures that every person in this country gets an equal opportunity.

The Democrat leaders have for decades wanted to gift those in the black community opportunities for votes as well as trying to have control over them. They have intentionally not allowed many of them to do things on their own.

It appears as if they are helping them, but again, they really just want to have control over them.

THOMASYOUNG

CHAPTER TEN

Fortunately, many of the Black Americans who have succeeded in life have overcome the Democratic leaders obstacles and have proudly made good lives for themselves.

Unfortunately though, there are still many more that are yearning to make it on their own merit, but are told by the left that the only way is to accept what they are given instead of what they earn.

Republicans have more faith that every American, regardless of skin color, can make it with an equal opportunity, instead of a biased system where one gets an opportunity based on checking a box instead of merit.

Another way that the Democrats have turned their backs to Black Americans is how they have prioritized illegal immigrants and have shoved

Black Americans aside.

Like in other cases, most Republicans would like to have legal residents here and have the money that's spent on illegal immigrants to go to some of the earlier mentioned programs that have helped Black Americans.

Now, switching gears to something that has haunted the black community for not just years but decades, is a subject that is deeply dividing. This subject is abortion. This isn't taking a side one way or another but is just stating some facts.

Planned Parenthood was started by Democrat Margaret Sanger, who was a very large racist.

Every year approximately 600,000 (or more) babies are aborted with a very large disproportionate number belonging to Black Americans.

According to the National Library of Medicine black women have been receiving abortions at an astounding 4 times the rate of white women.

This government site also states that this has been going on for at least 3 decades and very possibly much longer.

Just think of the tens of millions of Black children that were never born.

The Democrat leaders seem to have no problem limiting the number of Black Americans in this country.

The Republicans want them to not only be here but

to thrive as well.

Democrats think that easier access to contraceptives is the answer. The problem with that notion is that there are already an abundance of women's clinics where they can get contraceptives, many at no cost, but the abortions keep on coming.

Again, the Republicans don't want to use these Black women as political tools, sacrificing future Black children to fit an agenda.

They want as many as possible to survive and thrive.

Also, the number of Black families with two parents has plummeted from decades ago.

Democrat leaders see nothing wrong with this ,whereas Republicans know that statistically speaking, two parent households raise kids that are less likely to get into trouble. Time magazine published a story in September of 2023 that reinforced these claims.

There are still more ways that the Democratic leaders continue to hurt, sometimes literally, those in the black community.

Crime numbers in the Democrat run cities are appalling. The number of senseless deaths are heartbreaking.

In many cases they want to give criminals cashless bail so that they can continue to bring harm to minorities in the inner cities.

This makes zero logical sense, but they do it anyway.

Republicans want to take the criminals off of the streets and make all of the communities in the inner cities safer for everyone.

Often times the Democrats, and the media distort the truth and even flat out lie to further their agendas.

The truth isn't always pretty, but needs to be told if we are ever going to fix the problems.

The crime numbers are often not what they are being portrayed. The actual statistics from the FBI/DOJ Database bears this out.

Most homicides are either black on black or white on white.

There is a disproportionate number of homicide assailants that are black compared to white or Hispanic.

A large number of these can be attributed to gangs in the inner cities.

This begs the question, why don't we get extra cops to take the criminals off of the streets and make it safer for the residents there?

Other statistics show that contrary to what is told by Democratic leaders and the media, there are far more black on white murders than white on black.

Also, even though it's rare, there are more white people than black killed by cops.

The number of unarmed victims also ends up being

more white people than black.

In addition to that, those numbers barely break double digits.

While one is too many, those numbers are not what one would expect to hear, especially with the way the mainstream media and the left sensationalize things to their own benefit.

Many of them want division as it keeps them in business.

Now, we just have to disregard the Democrat way of attempting to control people, especially those in the black community, and allow everyone to help themselves.

This allows every person, regardless of their skin color, to earn their way to endless opportunities!

Also, in the end it's good to remember that no matter what many of the Democratic leaders, or the mainstream media, try to tell you, the vast majority of all people in this country are good people that get along well with each other and want the best for everyone.

Unfortunately many leaders in this country, mostly Democrat, would rather have division, as that benefits themselves.

Then, there is the other side, led by Donald Trump, who in a speech on June 22, 2024, in Philadelphia, Pennsylvania, had a unifying message as he said, "The people of country are looking for hope.

Whether they are white, black, brown, or anything else, they're looking for hope".

That pretty much says it all. We're all in this together!

Printed in Great Britain
by Amazon